HURRICANE AT THE ZOO!

David Tetzlaff
as told to Michelle Parsons

Contents

Rigby®
A Harcourt Achieve Imprint

www.Rigby.com
1-800-531-5015

David Tetzlaff, Zoo Director

In 1969 my parents started a zoo at Caribbean Gardens in Naples, Florida. Today I'm the Zoo Director. But I have worked many kinds of jobs here at the zoo. My first job was cleaning the elephant cages.

This is me as a young boy.

Here I am taking care of a large snake.

I'm in charge of all the animals in our collection. It is my job to protect the animals and their habitats, or homes. I also direct the many people who work here.

A Powerful Storm Is Coming

Hurricane Wilma began at the eastern edge of the Atlantic Ocean on October 15, 2005. News reporters announced the storm nine days before it arrived. Reports said the hurricane would hit Mexico and then head toward Florida.

Did You Know?

▶ A hurricane is a storm with heavy rain and winds 75 miles per hour or stronger.

▶ Hurricanes cause flooding, building and road damage, phone and power outages, injuries, and death.

▶ Hurricanes start near the equator in either the Atlantic Ocean, Caribbean Sea, or eastern Pacific Ocean.

▶ Hurricanes range from Category 1, the weakest, to Category 5, the strongest. Hurricane Wilma was a Category 3 storm when it hit Florida on October 24, 2005.

I listened to the news and heard that Hurricane Wilma had battered Mexico. I was amazed by how long the storm stayed in one place! This gave our community and the zoo plenty of time to prepare for the storm.

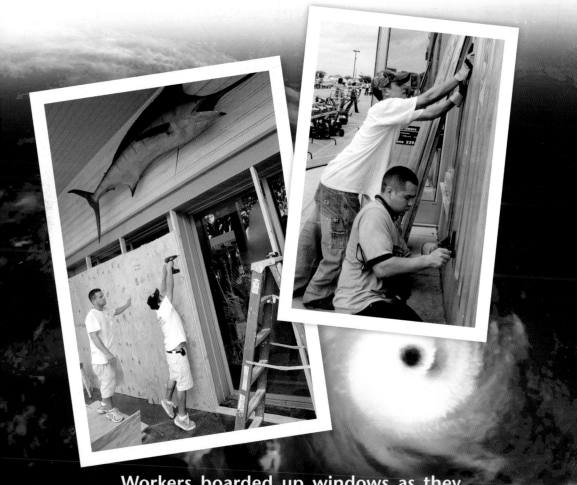

Workers boarded up windows as they prepared for Hurricane Wilma.

Preparation Begins

Preparing a zoo for a hurricane is a big job. We had to think about all 200 animals at the zoo. We have everything from poisonous snakes to giant elephants. Where would they all safely survive the storm?

Zoo Facts

▶ Naples Zoo is part of Caribbean Gardens, a 52-acre garden built in 1919.

▶ In 1969 David Tetzlaff's parents bought the garden, making it a home for their many wild animals.

▶ The zoo's 52-foot sign was a famous sight in South Florida until Hurricane Wilma destroyed it.

The winds from Hurricane Wilma were expected to be about 125 miles per hour. How could we protect the animal habitats? How would we prevent flooding? We also had to find a safe place to store things that might fly around in the wind. That meant finding safe places for everything from trash cans to tractors.

The animals at Naples Zoo get to enjoy a large natural setting.

Protecting the Animals

For two full days, we worked hard to prepare the animals for the storm. Each animal had to have shelter. We put the large and dangerous carnivores, or meat eaters, in concrete buildings with bars on the windows and locks on the doors. They needed lots of space.

Zoo workers move a tiger to a safe place before the storm.

We moved monkeys, small animals, birds, and reptiles into other safe buildings. But what did we do with the poisonous snakes? First we had to catch them! Then we put them in special cloth bags and protected them in locked crates.

Poisonous snakes needed extra care during the storm.

The animals would need to eat and drink during and after the storm. So we filled large plastic barrels with fresh water. We made sure we had extra fruit, vegetables, hay, grain, and meat for the animals. Then we set up generators, or back-up electricity boxes, for emergency power. This would help keep the food fresh.

Workers prepared fresh fruit and vegetables for the animals.

The animals needed to eat plenty
of food before the storm.

Protecting the Habitats and Zoo Grounds

Once the animals were safe, our biggest worry was that the hurricane would harm the outdoor habitats. We knew that if an animal's habitat was destroyed, we would have to find housing for the animal until the old one was repaired.

To protect the zoo grounds, we put away chairs, tables, trash cans, and tools. An area hit by a hurricane can be like a battlefield, and these items could be like flying weapons. We moved trucks to places where trees could not fall on them. We also put boards on windows and piled sandbags to prevent flooding.

We were as ready as we could be. I sent the workers home. Conrad Schmitt, another zoo manager, and I stayed at the zoo. We slept in the the zoo gift shop during the storm. We had food, water, flashlights, sleeping bags, and a radio. If the storm became unsafe, we had plans to move to another building with the animals.

Windows needed to be boarded up to protect the animals.

Surviving the Storm

The storm hit at about 6 A.M. on October 24, 2005. The wind roared, and sheets of rain lashed against the building. We opened the back door for only a minute and helplessly watched the wind peel the metal roof right off the reptile building.

It's hard to explain a hurricane to someone who has not experienced one, but the wind never seems to stop! The gift shop roof creaked, buckled, and moaned. We didn't sleep much that night!

Hurricane winds are incredibly powerful.

Heartbreaking Loss

After the storm ended, Conrad and I checked all the animals and buildings. The storm had left us with a heartbreaking loss! The leopard and wallaby exhibits were crushed, and the zoo's one-mile path was littered with fallen hedges, trees, and tree limbs.

The storm had harmed the wild dog and kangaroo habitats and many other exhibits. The wind had knocked down or shredded hundreds of trees, large and small. Some trees fell on fences that surrounded animals' homes. These would have to be repaired before the animals returned to their homes.

A Sad Moment

Thankfully no animals were killed during the storm. However, as we prepared for the storm, a wallaby and its baby died when workers tried to catch them. Most likely the stress was too much for them.

What to Do First

Once we saw all the wreckage, we started the generator to keep the meat freezer cold. Then we sent out teams to feed and give water to the animals. There were many things to do all at once!

NAPLES ZOO
at CARIBBEAN GARDENS

- Organize workers to make the best use of everyone's time.

- Make repairs to animal habitats.

- Fix sections of fence.

- Clear zoo path for trucks, tractors, and golf carts.

- Repair buildings and trim trees so zoo can safely reopen.

Asking for Help

The zoo sent a letter to news organizations. It said the zoo would be closed for at least a month. Dozens of volunteers arrived to help. They removed trash, cut fallen trees, and raked enormous piles of leaves.

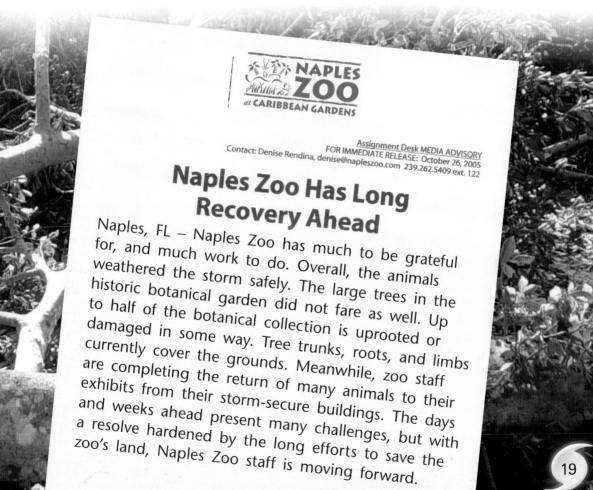

NAPLES ZOO
at CARIBBEAN GARDENS

Assignment Desk MEDIA ADVISORY
FOR IMMEDIATE RELEASE: October 26, 2005
Contact: Denise Rendina, denise@napleszoo.com 239.262.5409 ext. 122

Naples Zoo Has Long Recovery Ahead

Naples, FL – Naples Zoo has much to be grateful for, and much work to do. Overall, the animals weathered the storm safely. The large trees in the historic botanical garden did not fare as well. Up to half of the botanical collection is uprooted or damaged in some way. Tree trunks, roots, and limbs currently cover the grounds. Meanwhile, zoo staff are completing the return of many animals to their exhibits from their storm-secure buildings. The days and weeks ahead present many challenges, but with a resolve hardened by the long efforts to save the zoo's land, Naples Zoo staff is moving forward.

Expensive Repairs Ahead

The Naples Zoo is a non-profit organization. Our budget, or the money we use to run the zoo, comes from people and businesses. Raising money to rebuild habitats is our biggest challenge.

Even our sign needed to be fixed.

Rebuilding after the hurricane will be very expensive. It costs hundreds of thousands of dollars to create new animal displays. We hope to raise enough money to replace destroyed buildings with new buildings that will stand up against hurricanes.

It will take a long time to rebuild parts of the zoo.

Lessons Learned

Hurricanes can be very dangerous. People need to take these types of storms seriously.

It's normal to be afraid. I was! But the best way to deal with fear is with common sense and good preparation.

Traffic often gets backed up when everyone tries to leave quickly before a hurricane.

When a hurricane is coming, many people have the chance to evacuate, or quickly leave. Because the animals had to stay, I did, too. With preparation, we survived the hurricane and we continue the recovery efforts.

Index